WHAT YOU NEVER KNEW ABOUT LIONEL MESSI

by Isaac Kerry

CAPSTONE PRESS
a capstone imprint

This is an unauthorized biography.

Spark is published by Capstone Press, an imprint of Capstone
1710 Roe Crest Drive, North Mankato, Minnesota 56003
capstonepub.com

Library of Congress Cataloging-in-Publication Data
Names: Kerry, Isaac, author.
Title: What you never knew about Lionel Messi / by Isaac Kerry.
Description: North Mankato, Minnesota : Capstone, [2023] | Series: Behind the scenes biographies | Includes bibliographical references and index. | Audience: Ages 9-11 | Audience: Grades 4-6 | Summary: "Lionel Messi is a superstar soccer player. But what happens when he's not scoring goals on the pitch? High-interest details and bold photos of his fascinating life will enthrall reluctant and struggling readers, while carefully leveled text will leave them feeling confident"— Provided by publisher.
Identifiers: LCCN 2022024636 (print) | LCCN 2022024637 (ebook) | ISBN 9781669003090 (hardcover) | ISBN 9781669040590 (paperback) | ISBN 9781669003052 (pdf) | ISBN 9781669003076 (kindle edition)
Subjects: LCSH: Messi, Lionel, 1987—Juvenile literature. | Soccer players—Argentina—Biography—Juvenile literature. | Futbol Club Barcelona—History—Juvenile literatrue. | Paris-Saint-Germain-Football-Club—History—Juvenile literatrue.
Classification: LCC GV942.7.M398 K45 2023 (print) | LCC GV942.7.M398 (ebook) | DDC 796.334092 [B]—dc23/eng/20220509
LC record available at https://lccn.loc.gov/2022024636
LC ebook record available at https://lccn.loc.gov/2022024637

Editorial Credits
Editor: Erika L. Shores; Designer: Heidi Thompson; Media Researcher: Jo Miller; Production Specialist: Tori Abraham

Image Credits
Alamy: Aflo Co. Ltd., 11, ARCHIVIO GBB, 16, PA Images, 21, WENN Rights Ltd, 12; Associated Press/Luca Bruno, 19; Getty Images: Aurelien Meunier, 25, Gabriel Rossi, 22, Shaun Botterill, Cover; Newscom: pressinphoto/Sipa USA, 27; Shutterstock: A.RICARDO, 13, A.Taoualit, 4, 29, Bodor Tivadar, 8, charnsitr, 28, Christian Bertrand, 14, Jesus Cervantes, 18, ph.FAB, 15, Romain Biard, 7, Serg64, 20, Suthin _Saenontad, 26, Ververidis Vasilis, 9, worapan kong, 23

All internet sites appearing in back matter were available and accurate when this book was sent to press.

Printed in the United States 5769

TABLE OF CONTENTS

Words in **bold** are in the glossary.

THE BEST IN THE WORLD

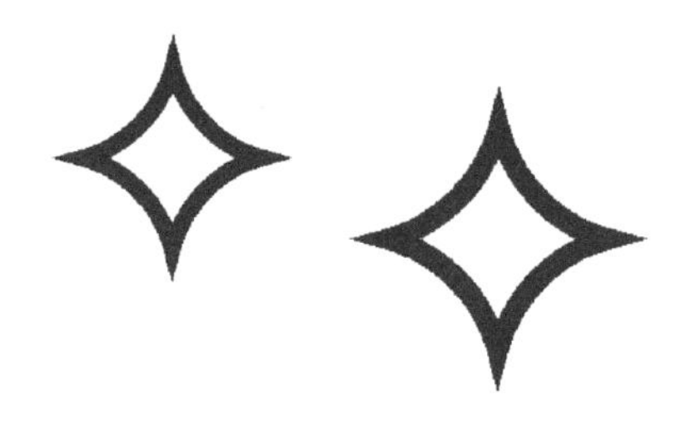

What does it take to be the best soccer player? Does a player need to score the most goals? Be the greatest at passing? What about moving the ball past defenders?

Lionel Messi makes answering this question easy. He is the best at ALL parts of the game. Many people say he's the GOAT, or the Greatest Of All Time.

FACT

Lionel also goes by the nickname Leo.

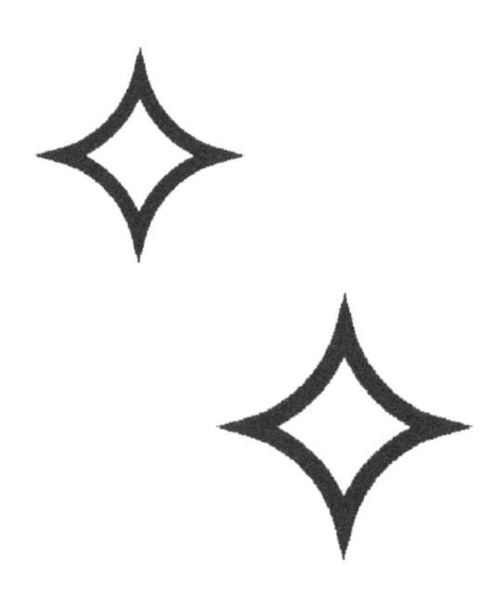

ALL ABOUT MESSI

Think you know what makes Leo Messi tick?

Take this quiz to find out!

1. **What is his favorite color?**
2. **What is his favorite type of music?**
3. **When is Lionel's birthday?**
4. **How old was he when he played his first official match for FC Barcelona?**

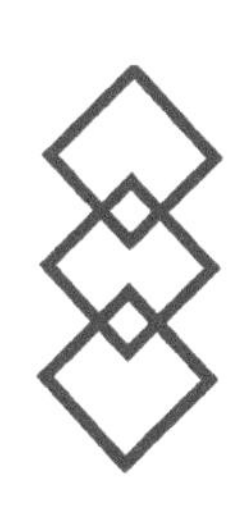

1. Red **2.** Cumbia **3.** June 24, 1987 **4.** 17 years old

LIONEL MESSI BY THE NUMBERS

Leo is 5 feet, 7 inches tall. He's shorter than many other soccer players. But that doesn't slow him down! Early in his career, he earned the nickname La Pulga. This means "the flea" in Spanish. Fleas are famously fast!

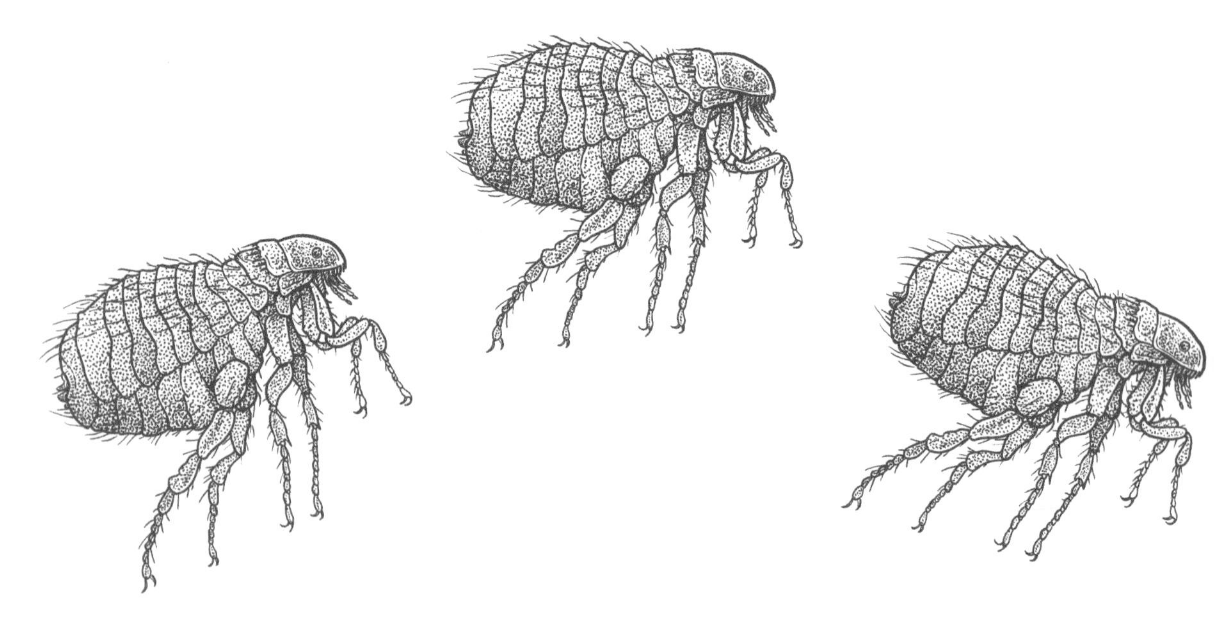

Rakuten

Lionel is one of the highest paid athletes in the world. He made $110 million during the 2021–2022 season.

It's not only his skills that are worth serious cash. In 2013, a jeweler in Japan wanted to honor Leo. He made a statue of Lionel's foot. It was made of solid gold. Its price tag was $5.25 million.

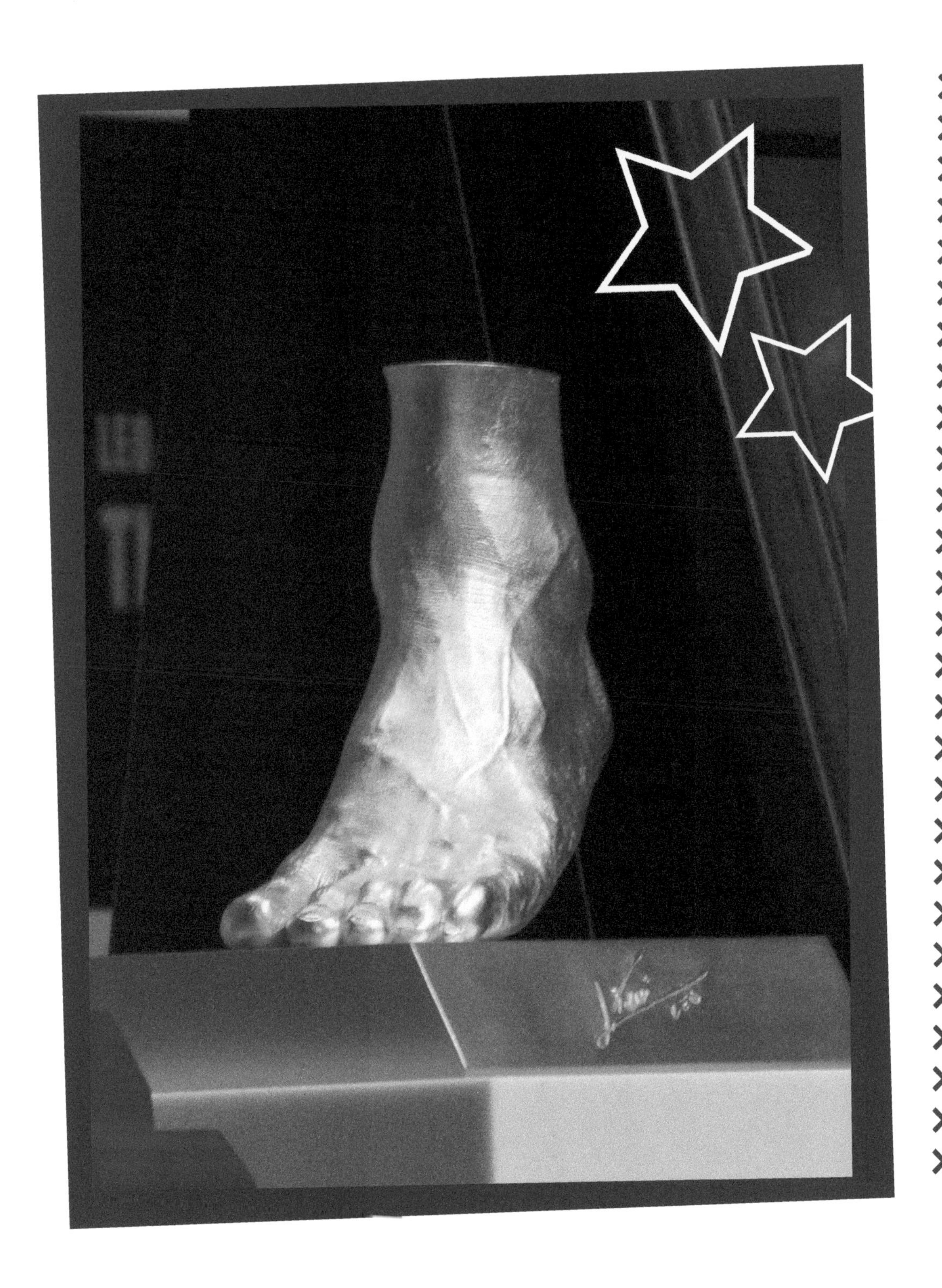

SO MANY GOALS
SO LITTLE TIME

Leo has a huge list of records. He leads his soccer **league** in all-time scores. From 2004 to 2021, he scored 474 times. The next highest number is only 311! He also leads in **assists** as well as match wins.

Whenever Lionel scores a goal, he celebrates the same way. He raises both hands and points to the sky. He **dedicates** the goal to his grandmother's memory. She brought him to his first soccer game.

MESSI
10

GROWING UP

At age 11, doctors found out Leo had a growth problem. He needed expensive medicine.

Luckily, Leo was already showing his skills on the field. A Spanish soccer club offered to pay for his medicine. But Leo's family would have to move from Argentina to Spain. Leo's parents made the choice to move their family.

FACT

An employee of the team wanted to hire Lionel as soon as he saw him play. He wrote a **contract** on a napkin for Lionel to sign.

In the 2008 Olympics, Lionel played for his home country of Argentina. He scored two goals during their matches. He also set up the game-winning assist in the gold medal match.

"The Olympic gold in 2008 is the win that I value the most because it is a tournament that you may play only once in your life..."

—Lionel Messi (*Spanish Esquire*, 2017)

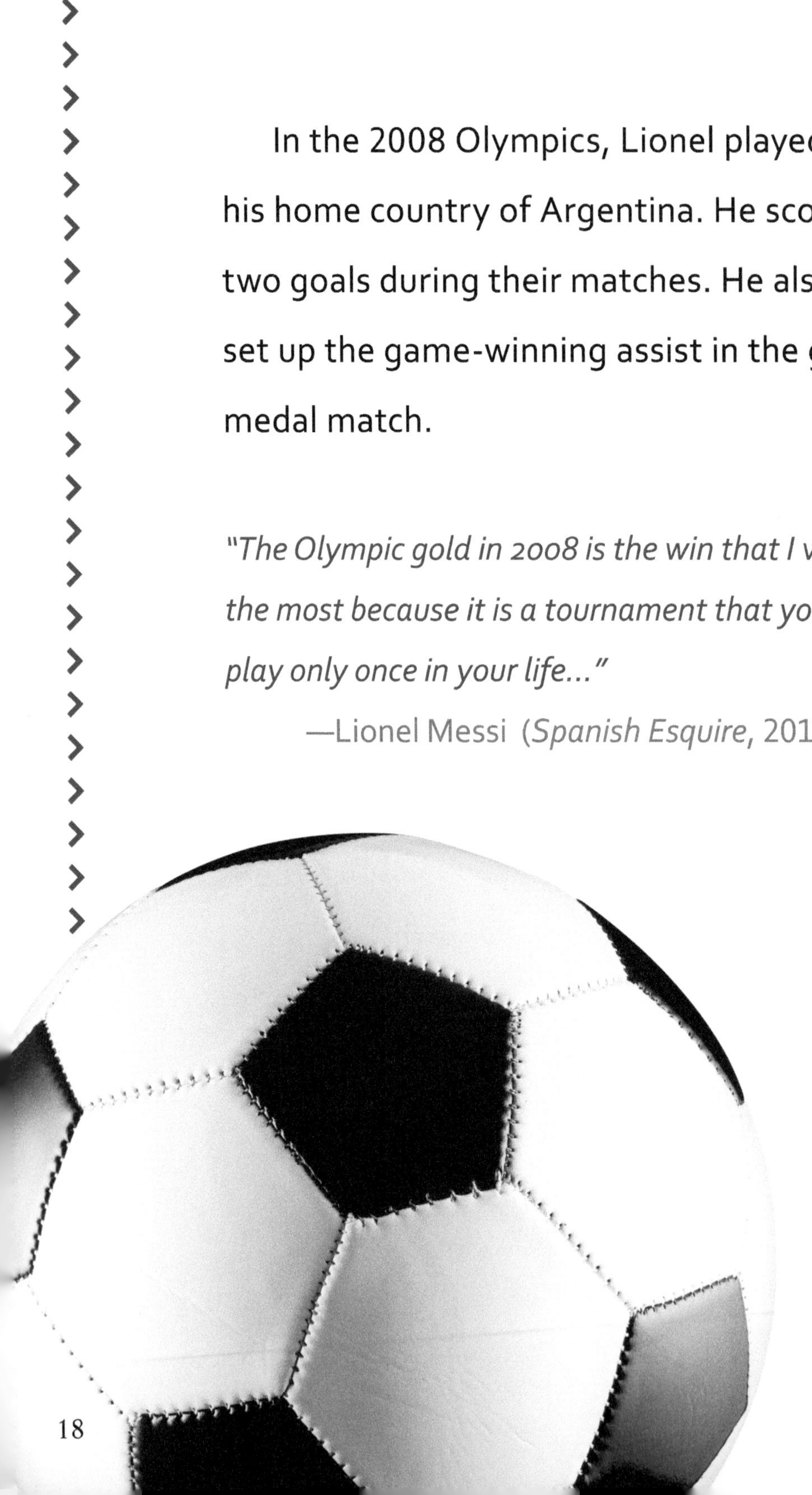

Leo used to eat a lot of junk food. That diet did not help him on the field. He would throw up during matches.

In 2014, Leo decided to make a change. He worked with a sports doctor. Leo needed to focus on eating fruits and vegetables. He drank more water and cut out soda. Leo started feeling better. He stopped throwing up during games.

POWERADE

FAMILY TIME

Lionel is married to his childhood sweetheart, Antonela Roccuzzo. She is the cousin of one of his best friends. They first met when they were only 5.

Leo and Antonela's wedding was described as the "wedding of the century" in Argentina. It was filled with famous celebs and soccer stars.

Lionel and Antonela have three sons. Their names are Thiago, Mateo, and Ciro. Thiago has also started to play soccer. Maybe he will be the next Messi superstar.

FACT

Lionel has his sons' names tattooed on his right leg.

"Having three children changed my perspective on life, my way of thinking, and it also helped me grow."

—Lionel Messi (*Marca*, 2019)

FRANCE FOOTBALL
L'EQUIPE
socios.com
WMH
PURNELL
PARIONS SPORT

Family time is important to Leo. He loves having breakfast with his kids and wife. They go on lots of fun vacations too. Antonela posts about them online. Some of their favorite spots are islands in Spain and the Caribbean.

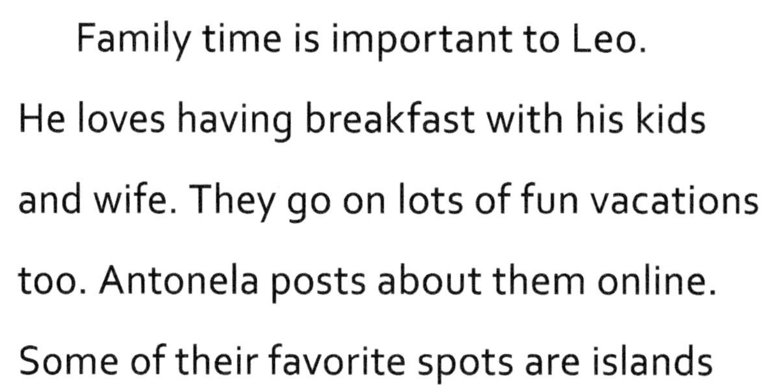

FACT

Besides soccer, Lionel enjoys tennis and padel. Padel is like a combination of tennis and squash.

beko
10

Leo and his family moved to Paris in the summer of 2021. He signed a two-year contract to play for Paris Saint-Germain.

Leo says his family enjoys the city but not the weather. It's wetter and cooler than in Spain. Who knows? Maybe Leo and his family will return to Spain in the future!

MESSI
30
LIGUE 1
Uber Eats
ooredoo
PARIS

Glossary

assist (uh-SIST)—a pass that leads to a score by a teammate

contract (khan-TRAKT)—an agreement to do something

dedicate (DED-uh-kate)—to set apart for a special reason

league (LEEG)—a group of teams that play against each other

Read More

Henderson, Brien. *FC Barcelona*. New York: Cavendish Square Publishing, 2021.

Jökulsson, Illugi. *Messi and Ronaldo: Who Is the Greatest?* New York: Abbeville Press Publishers, 2020.

Shoup, Kate. *Lionel Messi: Legendary Soccer Player*. New York: Cavendish Square, 2020.

Internet Sites

Lionel Messi
activityvillage.co.uk/lionel-messi

Lionel Messi
kids.britannica.com/students/article/Lionel-Messi/627581

Lionel Messi Facts for Kids
kids.kiddle.co/Lionel_Messi

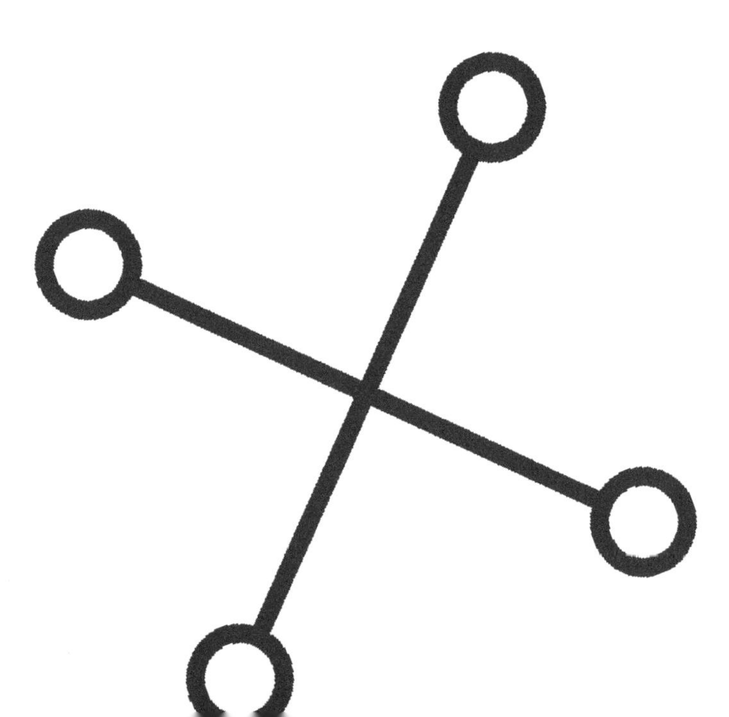

Index

About the Author

Isaac Kerry is an author, stay-at-home dad, and firefighter. He lives in Minnesota with his wife, two daughters, and an assortment of four-legged creatures. He can often be found writing, wrangling children, or riding big red trucks. In his all-too-limited free time he loves reading, working out, and playing board games.